I0880481

SandCastle™

Primeros Sonidos

Melina y Marcos

Cathy Camarena, M.Ed., and Gloria B. Ruff, M.Ed.

Consulting Editors

Lourdes Flores-Hanson, M.S.E., and Gloria Rosso-White

ABDO Publishing Company

capstone®

www.capstoneclassroom.com

Melina y Marcos © 2006 by Abdo Consulting Group, Inc. International copyrights reserved in all countries. This version distributed and published by Capstone Classroom © 2016 with the permission of ABDO. No part of this book may be reproduced in any form without written permission from the publisher. SandCastle™ is a trademark and logo of ABDO Publishing Company.

Credits
Curriculum Coordinator: Nancy Tuminelly
Cover and Interior Design and Production: Mighty Media
Child Photography: Steven Wewerka, Wewerka Photography
Photo Credits: AbleStock, Brand X Pictures, Photodisc

ISBN 978-1-4966-0355-5 (paperback)

Printed in the United States of America in North Mankato, Minnesota.
012015 008756

SandCastle™ books are created by a professional team of educators, reading specialists, and content developers around five essential components that include phonemic awareness, phonics, vocabulary, text comprehension, and fluency. All books are written, reviewed, and leveled for guided and early intervention reading, and designed for use in shared, guided, and independent reading and writing activities to support a balanced approach to literacy instruction.

SandCastle Level: Beginning

Mm

ABCChDEFGH
IJKLLLMNÑOP
QRSTUVWXYZ

abcchdefgh
ijklllmnñop
qrstuvwxyz

Melina

Marcos

mono

mosca

manzana

mitón

mapache

Aquí está el .

Aquí está la .

Aquí está la .

Aquí está el .

Aquí está el  .

A Marcos le gustan las manzanas.

La manzana es roja.

Melina también
tiene una manzana.

A la mosca le gusta
la manzana de
Melina.

Al mono le gustan las moscas y las manzanas.

¿Cuáles de estas cosas comienzan con **m**?

Más palabras que comienzan con m

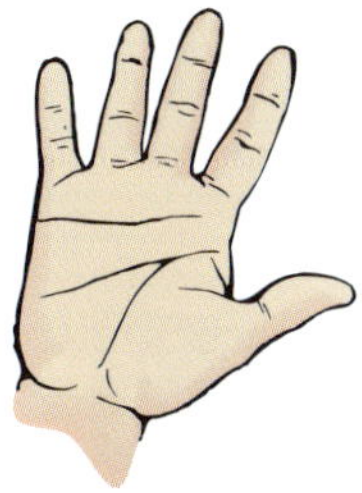

mano

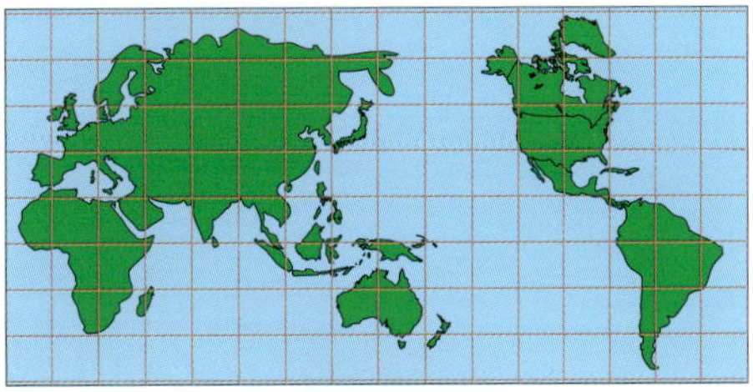

mapa

marcador

miel

mochila

About SandCastle™

A professional team of educators, reading specialists, and content developers created the SandCastle™ series to support young readers as they develop reading skills and strategies and increase their general knowledge. The SandCastle™ series has four levels that correspond to early literacy development in young children. The levels are provided to help teachers and parents select the appropriate books for young readers.

Emerging Readers
(no flags)

Beginning Readers
(1 flag)

Transitional Readers
(2 flags)

Fluent Readers
(3 flags)

These levels are meant only as a guide. All levels are subject to change.

ABDO Publishing Company
www.abdopub.com

capstone
www.capstoneclassroom.com